INVESTIGATING THE UNEXPLAINED

HAUNTED HOUSES

By Lisa Owings

BELLWETHER MEDIA • MINNEAPOLIS, MN

Blastoff! Discovery launches
a new mission: reading to learn.
Filled with facts and features, each
book offers you an exciting new
world to explore!

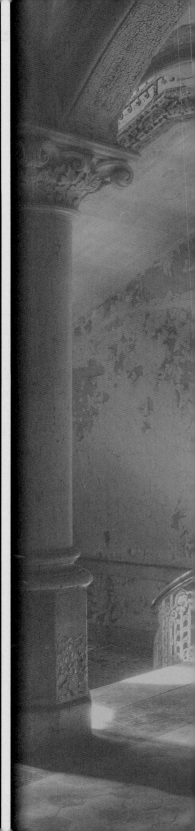

This edition first published in 2019 by Bellwether Media, Inc.

No part of this publication may be reproduced in whole or in
part without written permission of the publisher.
For information regarding permission, write to
Bellwether Media, Inc., Attention: Permissions Department,
6012 Blue Circle Drive, Minnetonka, MN 55343.

Library of Congress Cataloging-in-Publication Data

Names: Owings, Lisa, author.
Title: Haunted Houses / by Lisa Owings.
Description: Minneapolis, MN : Bellwether Media, Inc., 2019. |
   Series: Blastoff! Discovery: Investigating the Unexplained
   | Includes bibliographical references and index.
Identifiers: LCCN 2018003688 (print) | LCCN 2018008768
   (ebook) | ISBN 9781626178540 (hardcover : alk. paper)
   | ISBN 9781681035956 (ebook)
Subjects: LCSH: Haunted houses–Juvenile literature.
Classification: LCC BF1475 (ebook) | LCC BF1475 .O954
   2019 (print) | DDC 133.1/22–dc23

LC record available at https://lccn.loc.gov/2018003688

Editor: Paige Polinsky   Designer: Andrea Schneider

Printed in the United States of America, North Mankato, MN.

TABLE OF CONTENTS

A NOISE IN THE ATTIC

Amara has not had a good night's sleep in forever. Her family's new house still feels strange. Every night, the noise goes on for hours. It sounds like someone is pounding on her ceiling. Her mom blames the old pipes, but Amara is not so sure. She can feel something watching her, and it seems angry. Amara has to make her parents believe her.

REC

5

That night, the noise shakes the house. Amara watches her light swing back and forth. She can hear her parents in the hallway. Amara leaps out of bed and grabs her phone. She squeezes past her parents to race up the attic stairs.

Cracking the door, she shoves her hand in and watches the phone's camera flash go off. The noise stops instantly. Her parents gasp at the image on her screen. It reveals a dark shape with glowing eyes. Is a ghost haunting their house?

SECRET KEEPERS

Houses keep us safe and guard our secrets. But some have secrets of their own. People living there experience things they cannot explain. They may hear strange sounds or glimpse shadowy figures. Sometimes they become so frightened that they move away.

Many believe these experiences are caused by restless ghosts, or spirits, who died in the house or want something from its owners. They believe these houses are haunted.

COMMON HAUNTING SIGNS
- lights turn on and off on their own
- certain areas suddenly become cold
- unexplained shadows or lights
- unexplained sounds or smells
- objects move on their own
- pets act strangely

FAMOUS HAUNTED HOUSES IN THE UNITED STATES

1. Lemp Mansion – Missouri
2. Hickory Hill Mansion – Illinois
3. Winchester Mystery House – California
4. Myrtles Plantation – Louisiana
5. Whaley House – California
6. LaLaurie Mansion – Louisiana
7. Stranahan House – Florida
8. The White House – Washington D.C.
9. Hull House – Illinois
10. Amityville House – New York

REC

A HAUNTED HISTORY

Haunted houses have spooked us as far back as ancient Rome. Pliny the Younger wrote the earliest known account around the first century CE. Ghost encounters continued through the centuries. But people did not **investigate** hauntings until much later.

PLINY'S GHOST STORY

In Pliny's records, a noisy ghost appeared to a man renting a house. The ghost led him to a spot in the yard. Later, the man hired workers to dig there. They found bones and buried them properly. The ghost was never seen again.

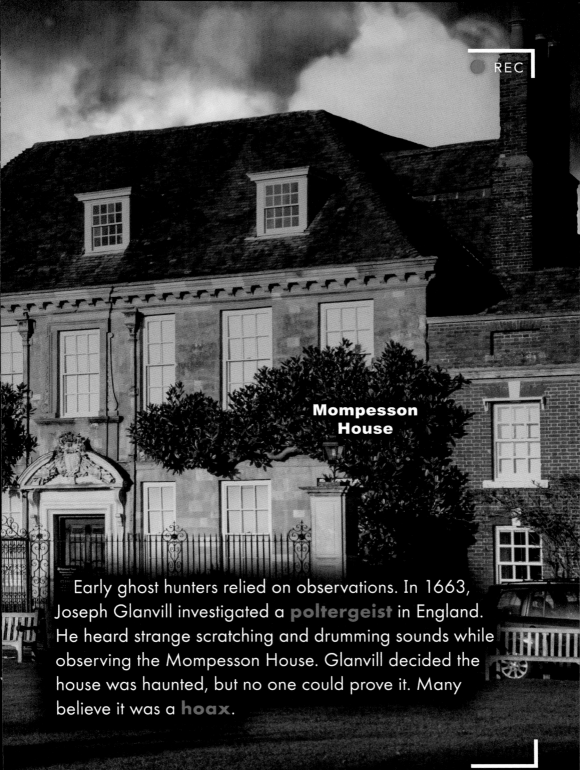

Mompesson House

Early ghost hunters relied on observations. In 1663, Joseph Glanvill investigated a **poltergeist** in England. He heard strange scratching and drumming sounds while observing the Mompesson House. Glanvill decided the house was haunted, but no one could prove it. Many believe it was a **hoax**.

the Fox sisters

Fox family home

In the 1800s, interest in hauntings exploded. Investigators turned to clairvoyance. They worked with mediums like the Fox sisters. Margaret and Kate Fox claimed to speak with spirits in their haunted New York home through knocking patterns. They toured the country with their sister, Leah. The Foxes convinced many that mediums could talk to ghosts haunting homes.

The Society for **Psychical** Research (SPR) was founded in 1882. Its members investigated the **paranormal**. One group observed haunted houses and questioned witnesses. They **debunked** many hauntings. But there were still cases they could not explain.

THE WINCHESTER MYSTERY HOUSE

After Sarah Winchester's husband died in 1881, she visited a medium. The medium warned that her family was cursed by ghosts. Sarah spent the rest of her life building a topsy-turvy mansion. Some say its mazes of rooms, dead-end stairs, and secret passages were meant to confuse angry spirits.

In 1929, SPR member Harry Price began investigating the Borley Rectory in England. His scientific approach made him one of the first famous ghost hunters. Price's ghost-hunting kit included **infrared** (IR) cameras, thermometers, and tools to measure air movement.

Ghost-hunting television shows became popular in the late 1990s. On these shows, investigators often visit concerned homeowners. They set up cameras and **audio recorders** at each house. They also measure temperature and **electromagnetic fields** (EMF). Then they review the data. Some investigators want to debunk hauntings. Others hope to prove them.

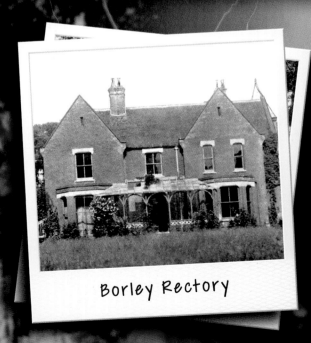

Borley Rectory

Ghost Hunters
TV show

REC

GOING IN

Today, there are many high-tech tools used to investigate hauntings. Video and still cameras are key for recording visible proof. Some cameras use IR technology to capture images in the dark. Many investigators use camera stands to film the most haunted areas overnight.

ARE YOU AFRAID OF THE DARK?

Most ghost hunts take place in low light for fewer distractions. But it is a myth that most ghosts come out at night. Sightings happen during the day, too!

INVESTIGATOR TOOLBOX

video camera   **audio recorder**   **motion detector**

IR thermometer   **EMF meter**

Motion detectors prevent hours of uneventful footage. Devices like cameras, alarms, and lights use them. Night-vision models are triggered any time IR levels spike. Other motion detectors use sound waves or lasers. When something disturbs these signals, the device switches on.

EMF meter

Many investigators believe ghosts cause cold spots. An IR thermometer can check the temperature of objects from a distance. This helps investigators find normal explanations for cold spots, like air vents. **Thermal cameras** scan larger areas. Their screens show temperatures as different colors. Sometimes strange outlines appear. These might belong to ghosts!

A popular **theory** says ghosts cause changes in electromagnetic fields. An EMF meter detects these changes. Electric currents move through its antenna. The meter tracks changes in the currents. Odd EMF readings might suggest a ghostly presence.

HOW INFRARED THERMOMETERS WORK

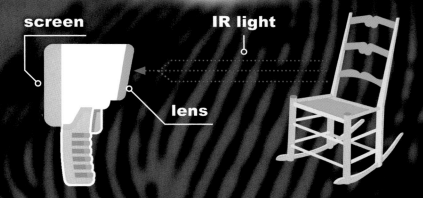

screen

IR light

lens

1. **All objects give off infrared light. A lens focuses this light onto a sensor called a thermopile.**

2. **The thermopile turns the light into heat. It then turns the heat into electricity.**

3. **A different sensor measures this electricity. It displays the amount as a temperature on the screen.**

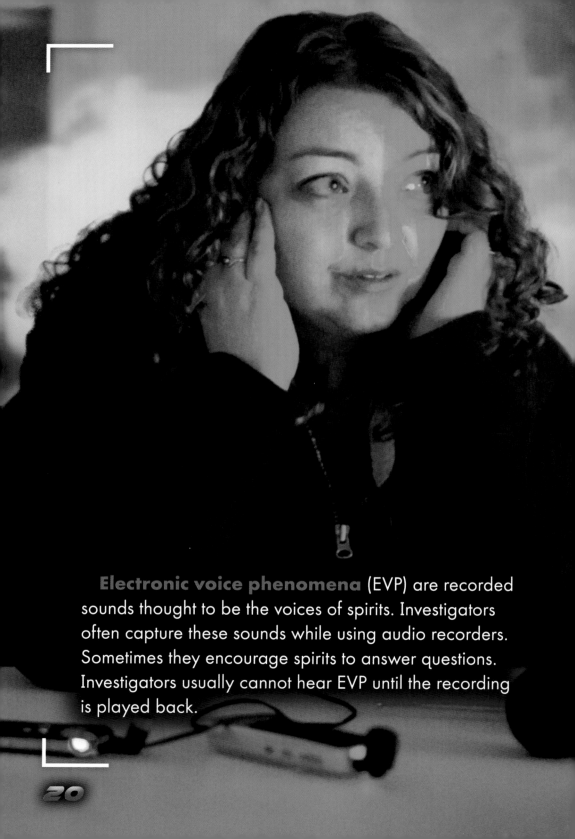

Electronic voice phenomena (EVP) are recorded sounds thought to be the voices of spirits. Investigators often capture these sounds while using audio recorders. Sometimes they encourage spirits to answer questions. Investigators usually cannot hear EVP until the recording is played back.

SOUND EDITING

Special computer programs help people see
anything unusual in their sound files. Most
programs can improve sounds by increasing
their volume or changing their speed.

The best audio recorders screen out background noise.
These cancel out any sound outside the normal range of
human voices. Investigators believe this helps them hear
ghosts rather than ceiling fans!

Amityville Horror House

PROFILE: THE AMITYVILLE HORROR HOUSE

In 1974, a family died in their home in Amityville, New York. A year later, the Lutzes moved in. They noticed awful smells and strange noises. The terrified family soon moved out.

Paranormal investigators Ed and Lorraine Warren were called to the scene. They sensed evil spirits using clairvoyance. They also took photos. One seemed to show the spirit of a little boy. Amityville became famous. Later, investigator Stephen Kaplan studied the case. After visiting the house, he found no **evidence** of a haunting. Kaplan and others claimed Amityville was a hoax.

Ed and Lorraine Warren

Stephen Kaplan

KAPLAN'S CASE

Stephen Kaplan directed the Parapsychology Institute of America, a paranormal research group. He used tools like IR cameras and thermometers to study the Amityville house. Kaplan's test results were normal. He also found that the home's doors and windows did not match the Lutzes' story.

HAUNT OR HOAX?

Skeptics believe there is no such thing as a haunted house. They say even the spookiest experiences have normal explanations. Strange noises are more likely to be caused by scurrying mice or the house sinking slightly. A strong draft could cause cold spots and blow things around.

dust or spirits?

Even technology can be fooled. Common devices like power outlets can throw off EMF readings. Weird lights, often from camera flashes bouncing off dust, can easily be mistaken for proof of spirits.

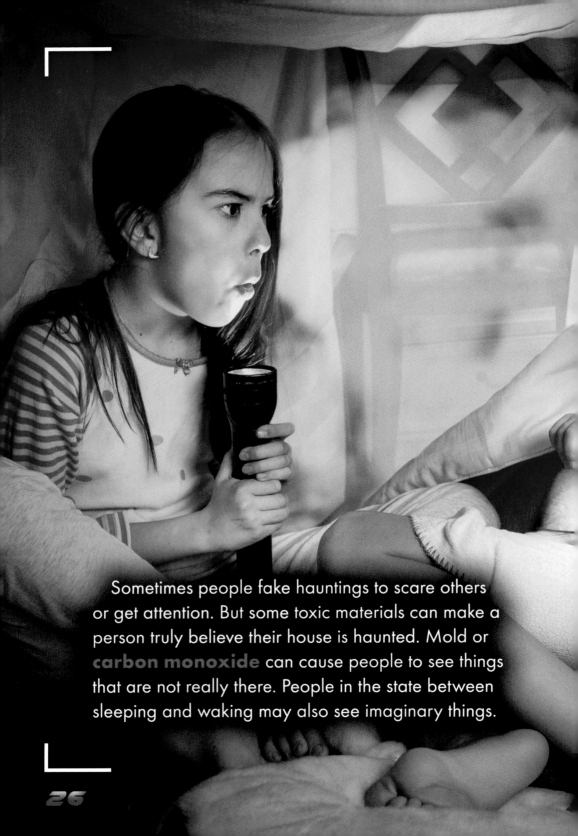

Sometimes people fake hauntings to scare others or get attention. But some toxic materials can make a person truly believe their house is haunted. Mold or **carbon monoxide** can cause people to see things that are not really there. People in the state between sleeping and waking may also see imaginary things.

Another theory says people have experiences that match their beliefs. If someone believes a house is haunted, they are more likely to see signs of spirits. Their imagination may give normal events ghostly meanings.

DO YOU BELIEVE?

Most haunted houses are not haunted at all. Even strong believers can usually find ordinary explanations for creepy houses. But several well-known haunts are open to the public. People seeking the truth about strange experiences can take tours to decide for themselves.

There are still things current science cannot explain, and that means some hauntings could be real. Do spirits truly roam the halls of some houses, or is there another explanation? What do you believe?

HAVE YOU HEARD?

Infrasound is sound below the normal range of human hearing. It can cause people to see or feel strange things. Studies suggest people who have heard infrasound are more likely to report ghost sightings.

REC

29

GLOSSARY

audio recorders—devices that capture and save sounds

carbon monoxide—a poisonous gas that has no smell or color

clairvoyance—the ability to feel things outside the five senses; clairvoyance often includes communicating with spirits or knowing events that will happen in the future.

debunked—revealed something as false

electromagnetic fields (EMF)—forces caused by the movement of electricity that create magnetic energy

electronic voice phenomena (EVP)—strange sounds on electronic recordings believed to be spirit voices

evidence—information that helps prove or disprove something

footage—video recordings

hoax—an act meant to fool or trick someone

infrared (IR)—concerned with energy that cannot be seen; infrared energy can be felt as heat.

investigate—to try to find out the facts about something in order to learn if or how it happened

mediums—people who claim they can communicate with spirits

paranormal—strange events or powers that cannot be explained by what is known about the world

poltergeist—a mischievous spirit that makes loud noises and throws objects

psychical—psychic; psychic people have powers of the mind that cannot be explained by science.

skeptics—people who doubt something is true

theory—an idea based on known facts that is meant to explain something

thermal cameras—cameras that can pick up on and show heat

TO LEARN MORE

AT THE LIBRARY

Bodden, Valerie. *Haunted Houses.* Mankato, Minn.: Creative Education, 2018.

McCollum, Sean. *Handbook to Ghosts, Poltergeists, and Haunted Houses.* North Mankato, Minn.: Capstone Press, 2017.

Oachs, Emily Rose. *Ghosts.* Minneapolis, Minn.: Bellwether Media, 2019.

ON THE WEB

Learning more about haunted houses is as easy as 1, 2, 3.

1. Go to www.factsurfer.com.

2. Enter "haunted houses" into the search box.

3. Click the "Surf" button and you will see a list of related web sites.

With factsurfer.com, finding more information is just a click away.

INDEX

The images in this book are reproduced through the courtesy of: Sergey Shubin, front cover (woman); Vinterriket, front cover; Grischa Georgiew, pp. 2-3; kryzhov, pp. 4-5, 26-27; pabbles, pp. 6-7; Ppictures, pp. 8-9; Russell Hoban/ Alamy, pp. 10-11; Library of Congress/ Wikipedia, p. 12 (top); Library of Congress/ Getty, p. 12 (bottom); Africa Studio, pp. 12-13; Charles Walker Collection/ Alamy, p. 14 (inset); Syfy/ Getty, pp. 14-15; Roberts Vicups, pp. 16-17; Orlando Sentinel/ Getty, pp. 18-19; Portland Press Herald, pp. 20-21; Bettmann/ Getty, pp. 22-23 (insets); Jim Bowling/ AP Images, p. 24 (inset); Vasilyev Alexandr, pp. 24-25; Yupa Watchanakit, p. 25 (ghost); Vjacheslav Shishlov, pp. 28-29.